Fearless Futures

A Mindful Approach to Consulting Services

Table of Contents

Chapter 1. Introduction

Welcome to "Fearless Futures: A Mindful Approach to Consulting Services," your ticket to an inspiring journey into the world of trailblazing business transformations. This eagerly-awaited Special Report unravels the innovative merger of analytical consulting models with mindfulness practices. It serves as a compass directing you towards an exciting new frontier, where ego-less leadership, co-creative collaboration, and client-centered solutions prevail, fostering paradigms of continuous growth and sustainable success. Let this vibrant guide inspire you to reimagine the possibilities, recalibrate your strategies, and invigorate your teams. One peek will leave you yearning to own this dynamic transformation tool. Embrace tomorrow's consulting norms today! Hurry, your fearless future awaits.

Chapter 2. Decoding the Language of Tomorrow: Introduction to Mindful Consulting

The 'Decoding the Language of Tomorrow: Introduction to Mindful Consulting' chapter begins as follows:

In the fast-paced world of business consulting, clients seek strategies that can navigate through their complex issues and lead to sustainable success. Mindful consulting emerges as a unique approach combining the rigors of scientific methodology with the empathic intelligence of mindfulness.

2.1. Understanding Mindful Consulting

Mindful consulting grounds its roots in the philosophy of mindfulness – the state of being present, aware, and without judgment. The approach aims to instill mindfulness in every aspect of consulting, creating a paradigm shift towards fostering open-mindedness, empathy, and mutual respect.

Fused with traditional consulting models, mindful consulting integrates comprehensive data analysis with conscious awareness of the clients' specific needs, dynamics, and challenges. It does not treat businesses merely as profit-generating mechanisms but as living systems composed of people expressing themselves through their roles and relationships.

2.2. The Ever-Evolving Consulting Canvas

The consulting world is a canvas that is constantly diversifying and evolving. Old consulting models no longer suffice—businesses demand more than just black-and-white data analyses. They yearn for solutions tailored to their holistic needs, considering the intricate human dynamics that underlie every organization.

Mindful consulting paints this canvas with a palette of introspection, empathy, and communication. It does not shun but rather welcomes the 'gray areas', using them as platforms for client-centered solutions. This departure from conventional methodologies paves the way for a richer, happier, and more sustainable environment for organizations.

2.3. Pillars of Mindful Consulting

Just like any robust structure, mindful consulting rests on strong pillars, each of them playing a crucial role in maintaining balance and continuity. These pillars are:

1. Mindfulness: Being completely present and consciously aware.
2. Compassion: Showcasing empathic understanding towards clients and their concerns.
3. Co-creation: Collaborating with clients to devise solutions.
4. Ego-less leadership: Guiding without arrogance, bias, or dominance.

Within these pillars, the consultant acts as a bridge, connecting the client's present reality to a visionary, sustainable future—built upon shared values, mutual respect, and a genuine regard for each other's perspectives.

2.4. Components of Mindful Consulting

Mindful consulting is made up of several components working concurrently:

2.4.1. Mindful Listening:

Attentive listening informs effective decision-making and enhances client relations. It includes picking up non-verbal cues, understanding both said and unsaid concerns, and genuinely appreciating the client's perspective.

2.4.2. Mindful Dialogue:

This involves promoting open, candid conversations. Encouraging honesty and transparency to squash any pretensions or hesitations, leading to authentic solutions.

2.4.3. Mindful Observation:

Observing the client's dynamics holistically, identifying interconnections, understanding underlying concerns, and recognizing patterns. This process goes beyond observation—it is an insightful exploration of the client's ecosystem.

2.4.4. Mindful Solutioning:

Creating solutions by combining analytical rigor and intuitive understanding. These solutions pivot around the client's core concerns and future aspirations.

2.5. The Future Of Consulting Lies In Mindfulness

Mindful consulting offers a transformative path in the realm of business consulting. The future belongs to these mindful consultants who can co-create innovative solutions that address both the rational and emotional dimensions of organizational issues. It invites consultants to journey deep into the heart and soul of every business, to truly decode the language of tomorrow.

The subsequent chapters will dive into the nuanced aspects of mindful consulting, from creating a mindful workspace to fostering an environment that cultivates innovation and empathetic leadership. Hold on tight, because we're about to embark on a journey that may very well redefine the way you think about consulting - a fearless future built on mindful practices. Let's continue this thrilling exploration, walking in step with the rhythm of the new age.

As we flip to the next chapter, envisage adopting a new lens to look at your client's business. See the people, understand the connections, value the rapport. See through the lens of mindfulness— it's more than a technique; it's a way of being. Let's dive into the world of mindful consulting, the language of tomorrow. Your blueprint to a fearless future begins here.

Chapter 3. Birth of Fearless Futures: The Emergence and Evolution

The genesis of Fearless Futures took place against the backdrop of a rapidly evolving business landscape. Amidst the increasing complexities and seemingly draconic challenges, there was a deep-seated need for an approach that transcended traditional analytical models and connected more deeply with the essence of businesses - its people.

3.1. From the Ashes of Traditional Consulting

Before we dive into the emergence of Fearless Futures, it is crucial to understand the landscape it was born out of. Traditional consulting services were heavily rooted in mechanical, formulaic strategies and didn't consider the unique human elements intrinsic to each organization. The prevailing modus operandi had consultants isolated from the teams they advised, with monetary performance metrics claiming the paramount importance. However, this approach began to show its flaws as businesses became more complex and the work environment more dynamic.

The standard models of problem-solving began to lag, unable to fully grasp and deal with growing uncertainties. Employees felt alienated, draining away morale and motivation. Clients often lacked satisfaction with generic, one-size-fits-all solutions. The seeds of change were sown amidst these turbulent times.

3.2. The Era of Change

The demand for a more holistic, mindful, and human-centric approach in consulting began to rise. This shift was led by forward-thinking executives who recognized the need for collaborative co-creation, diversity in thought, and an infusion of empathy into strategy formulation. These pioneers began to experiment, breaking down hierarchies, fostering cross-team communication and collaboration, and emphasizing the development and wellbeing of each team member. Slowly but surely, the status quo was changing.

3.3. The Emergence of Fearless Futures

The disruption caused by these trailblazing leaders paved the way for the emergence of Fearless Futures. Deriving its moniker from the vision of a future that welcomed change fearlessly, this new model sought to merge the analytical rigor of traditional consulting with mindfulness principles. The heart of this model lies in its commitment to create a harmonious blend of strategy and empathy, profit and people, thereby fostering a healthier, more sustainable business environment.

The novel approach encouraged consultants to no longer sit on the sidelines but to get hands-on, interacting with all layers of the company. It urged them to understand the unique challenges, perspectives, and aspirations of each team member, creating a more comprehensive view of the situation. Subsequently, this provided a deeper, more meaningful way of crafting strategies and solutions that were tailored to the organization's needs.

3.4. The Evolution of Fearless Futures

Like a seed sown in fertile soil, Fearless Futures began to grow, adapt and evolve. The initial phase of exploration and experimentation led to the development of a solid framework that placed equal emphasis on internal transformation and external growth. Key elements of mindfulness like non-judgement, acceptance, and presence became integral parts of this approach, fostering an environment that encouraged self-awareness, self-learning, and self-improvement.

With the advent of this novel methodology, businesses started experiencing more profound transformations. By breaking down silos and promoting connectivity and empathy within teams, solutions became organic, resonating with the needs and values of not just the business altogether, but the individuals within.

The evolution of Fearless Futures is still an ongoing journey as the model continuously adapts to the ever-changing landscape of the business world. By continuously learning and adapting, Fearless Futures is prepared to handle any challenge that the business environment may throw at it.

3.5. Looking Beyond Borders

Now more than ever, businesses are finding strength and value in the Fearless Futures approach to consulting services. As this new model continues to evolve, the future promises even greater opportunities and challenges. What remains secure is the commitment of Fearless Futures to foster environments where businesses can thrive fearlessly, ensuring a continuous journey of growth and sustainable success.

Chapter 4. In Pursuit of Balance: Integrating Mindfulness in Business Practices

Today's business world is marked by relentless pace, high stress, and overwhelming technological advancements. This continuous hustle indeed produces remarkable outcomes but also conceives an environment ripe for imbalance and burnout. Acknowledging this inherent conundrum, the solution does not strictly lie in detaching from our existing systems. We can forge a path forward by blending our modern practices with ancient antidotes. One of these antidotes, mindfulness, stands at the forefront of this transformation.

4.1. The Mindfulness Principle and Its Relevance

Mindfulness is the state of being conscious or aware of the present moment, which fosters an in-depth understanding of ourselves and our surroundings. Practicing mindfulness enables individuals to become non-judgmental listeners of their inner self, rooting their actions in deeper consciousness rather than mechanized reactions.

In business settings, mindfulness serves as a nexus between employees' wellbeing and organizational productivity. Researches suggest that mindful professionals exhibit higher job satisfaction, improved creativity, and advanced problem-solving skills; all instrumental in building a holistically sustainable business environment. Hence, integrating mindfulness principles in business practices is no longer an 'out-of-the-box' approach; it's becoming a 'must-have' for businesses eyeing long-term prosperity.

4.2. Embodying Mindfulness: Individual Perspective

Practicing mindfulness doesn't necessarily require major lifestyle changes or investing huge amounts of time or energy. It is more about adopting an attitude of conscious living. There are several ways in which individuals can cultivate mindfulness at work:

1. Prioritize simple mindfulness exercises: Deep breathing exercises, meditation, or yoga can serve as the crucial first steps.

2. Cultivate active listening: By completely focusing on the speaker without mentally crafting a response.

3. Embrace single-tasking: An antithesis to multitasking, concentrating on one task at a time enables more profound focus and reduced stress.

4. Regular breaks for digital detox: Providing relief from the near-constant interaction with screens.

4.3. Conscious Leadership: The Guiding Beacon

Leaders, as the architects of the corporate culture, shoulder the responsibility of creating an environment conducive to mindfulness. Ego-less leadership, a product of mindfulness, profoundly establishes the glory of humble, people-first orientation. Such leaders are empathetic, aware, and authentic, encouraging a culture where everyone is heard, understood, and respected.

1. Open communication: Leaders need to promote a platform that encourages clear, honest, and compassionate discussion.

2. Leading by example: Leaders themselves practicing mindfulness is the most potent demonstration of its importance.

3. Cultivating resilience: Mindful leaders lend stability even in times of crisis, encouraging resilience amongst the team members.

4. Active appreciation: Recognizing employees' efforts on a regular basis fuels their motivation and fosters a positive work environment.

4.4. Institutionalizing Mindfulness: Organizational Considerations

The actualization of a truly mindful organization demands systematic embedding of the mindfulness principle across its functions, systems, and culture. Following are some strategies:

1. Mindfulness training programs: These can provide tools and methodologies for employees to practice mindfulness.

2. Mindful meetings: Allocate a few minutes at the beginning or end of meetings for mindfulness exercises.

3. Work-life balance: Flexible working hours or remote working provision can create a balance enabling individuals to avoid burnout and stress.

4. Recognition and reward: Implementing systems to acknowledge and reward mindful behaviors would encourage more employees to practice the same.

4.5. The Mindful Shift: Potential Challenges and Solutions

As promising as it sounds, implementing mindfulness does come with its share of challenges, the most common being misconceptions and resistance to change. Hence, the pathway demands certain counter strategies:

1. Education and Awareness: Clear communication about the principles, benefits, and techniques of mindfulness helps reduce misconceptions.

2. Pilot Programs: Introduce mindfulness practices on a smaller scale initially and based on the feedback and success, extend it to the broader organization.

3. Regular Feedback: Feedback systems can help tweak strategies to make mindfulness integration more effective.

As we proceed towards an era characterized by information overload and accelerated changes, the harmony of mindfulness and business practices will prove to be more than just a trend – it's going to be a cornerstone of resilient, innovative, and humane organizations. This pursuit of balance in a chaotic world will empower individuals and organizations to convert their everyday struggles into enduring solutions, molding a business landscape that is exceptional, empathetic, and enlightened. Today, we stand at the this precipice. Will you take the leap into the fearless future? Your journey to a balanced, mindful business starts now.

Chapter 5. Beyond Borders: Embracing Global Collaboration and Diversity

In an interconnected world, the reliance on traditional consulting models has been challenged by the emergence of complex, global challenges. Here, we delve into a forward-thinking perspective, invoking the strategic advantages of integrating global collaboration and cultural diversity into contemporary consulting practices.

5.1. The Power of Global Collaboration

As firms recognize the edge that collaboration offers in tackling complex business issues, the potential rewards that come from tapping into diverse perspectives across geographical borders become evident. Forming global alliances not only fosters creative problem-solving but also caters to the growing consulting demands of multinational corporations.

Virtual technologies are, thus, strategic assets, enabling seamless, real-time interaction between team members spread across various locales. The key to success in global collaboration is encapsulated in the 'Three-C' Model: Communication, Coordination, and Co-creation.

Communication is the cornerstone of any collaborative effort. Emerging digital tools offer numerous channels to connect, confer, and consolidate ideas, facilitating the creation of rich, multi-layered dialogues. It's essential to establish transparent and open communication in all engagements.

Coordination is about aligning the efforts of distributed teams toward common goals, fostering efficiency, and driving project advancements. Identifying and communicating key milestones, timelines, and expected deliverables are crucial steps in this process.

Co-creation represents the pinnacle of global collaboration. Through the fusion of diverse skills, experience, and perspectives, innovative solutions can be birthed, pushing the boundaries of conventional thought and stimulating business growth.

5.2. Embracing Cultural Diversity

Diversity infuses novelty into consulting processes. A wealth of studies highlight the correlation between diverse teams and innovation, emphasizing the value of incorporating a plethora of cultural perspectives into problem-solving processes.

Diversity is multidimensional and includes factors beyond ethnicity and nationality, extending to age, gender, socio-economic backgrounds, professional experiences, and cognitive styles. Consultants should actively foster an environment of inclusion and respect, ensuring that all voices are heard and valued.

However, embracing diversity can present challenges. Differences in perception and interpretation could disrupt the smooth flow of ideas, leading to misunderstandings and conflicts. An effective solution lies in building cultural intelligence, the ability to bridge gaps, and negotiate cultural differences.

Cultural intelligence encompasses four key attributes:

1. **Cognitive:** Understanding the nuances of various cultures.

2. **Motivational:** A willingness to employ this understanding.

3. **Behavioral:** Ability to adapt behavior in line with cultural contexts.

4. **Metacognitive:** Reflecting and rehearsing before and after cross-

cultural interactions.

5.3. Integrating Collaboration and Diversity in Consulting Practices

At first glance, coordination of global efforts and an appreciation of cultural diversity might seem disparate. However, they are intertwined and mutually enforcing - each element amplifies the potential benefits of the other.

For instance, embracing diversity without effective coordination can lead to disarray, and collaborative efforts without diverse perspectives can lead to stagnation. It is the intersection of these elements where magic happens - where solutions attribute to varied perspectives and coordinated efforts.

Digital innovation supports this integration by creating platforms for interaction, innovation, and impact measurement. The key lies in choosing the right tools and setting clear guidelines for usage, drawn from the understanding of the 'Three-C' Model mentioned earlier.

5.4. Developing a Mindful Approach to Global Collaboration

Mindfulness is the missing link. As consultants embrace global collaboration, the higher cognitive load, time zone differences, etc., can lead to stress and burnouts. Mindfulness practices with focussing on the present moment without judgment offers a remedy.

Building a culture of mindfulness, one that encourages regular mental breaks, open dialogues about mental well-being, and non-judgmental mindfulness training sessions can fortify the mental resilience of consultants. It can foster their capacity to navigate the challenging terrains of global collaboration and cultural diversity with grace.

Global collaboration, cultural diversity, and mindfulness can usher in a new era of consulting practices. This synergy creates a fertile ground for growth, innovation, and unparalleled business success. Wield wisely, they promise to revolutionize consulting, opening doors to a future where consultants not only dissect business problems but also construct global solutions while embracing the richness of diversity and championing mental well-being. Welcome to the consulting of the future.

Chapter 6. You Reimagined: Unleashing the Power of Ego-less Leadership

Leadership stands as a cornerstone of any successful organization. It is through its leaders that an organization sets, pursues, and ultimately achieves its goals. However, traditional images of leadership often associate it with positions of power, authority, and control. Today, we implore you to reimagine leadership through a transformational perspective - an ego-less approach. This impressive chapter unwraps the dynamic connections between fearless leadership and mindfulness, guiding you through a journey that redraws the conventional boundaries of leadership roles.

6.1. Fearless Leadership: An Overdue Redefinition

Leaders have the potential to foster growth, change, and success, but these outcomes often build on a leader's personal power and authority. Welcome an overdue redefinition – Fearless Leadership. It promotes a selfless interpretation of leadership, pivoting the focus from a leader's personal ego and aggrandizement towards collective growth and success. Here, power is not merely a leader's tool to impact their subordinates; it is a shared resource that everyone within the team can access.

Ego-less Leadership exchanges 'command and control' management models for an innovative concept that embraces humility, authenticity, and empathy. It values collective contribution over individual stardom, echoing the mantra, "We are successful because we are united; we are powerful because we empower each other." It dismantles hierarchical barriers, fostering an atmosphere conducive to open communication, collaboration, and holistic development.

6.2. The Mindful Approach: Harnessing the Power of Now

Harnessing the power of 'now' is the essence of mindfulness. It is not just a therapeutic practice devoted to stress reduction or mental wellness. Mindfulness serves as a potent tool that amplifies the strength of fearless leadership. With the noise of personal ambition, rigid thinking, and judgement filtered out, leaders become more attuned to their surroundings, more aligned with their teams, and more focused on their organizational objectives.

Practicing mindful leadership empowers leaders to be present – fully aware, observant, and responsive – fostering an environment that celebrates innovation, resilience, and continuous learning. The Mindful Approach teaches leaders to de-emphasize past success or future ambition in favor of the invaluable lessons available in the present moment.

6.3. Embracing Vulnerability: The Catalyst for Authentic Relationships

When leaders let go of ego, they willingly remove their armor, inviting others to do the same and fostering a deeper, authentic connection. Embracing vulnerability does not equate to weakness. Rather, it is a powerful testament to the strength of one's character. It encourages open dialogue, the exchange of feedback, and the resultant growth of the team and its individual members.

As Brené Brown explains, "Vulnerability sounds like truth and feels like courage. Truth and courage aren't always comfortable, but they're never weakness." By inspiring trust and camaraderie through authentic relationships, leaders catalyze both personal and professional growth, laying the groundwork for enduring success.

6.4. The Alchemy of Empathy: Fostering Inclusive Workspaces

Empathy – the ability to understand and share the feelings of others – is the faithful companion of ego-less leadership. By tapping into collective emotions, leaders can create a bond that transcends the traditional confines of a professional relationship, uniting the team over shared feelings, concerns, and triumphs.

An empathetic leader creates a rippling effect of respect, caring, and compassion in the workplace. Such inclusive workspaces acknowledge diversity and respect the unique contributions of each team member, establishing a culture where everyone feels valued, appreciated, and integral to the team's success.

6.5. Co-Creative Collaboration: Unleashing Collective Genius

Ego-less Leadership embodies the spirit of co-creation, where every opinion matters, every contribution counts, and every person holds the power to positively impact organizational goals. It encourages open dialogue, shared decision-making, and mutual learning, converting a group of isolated professionals into a dynamic, co-creative team.

Co-creation dismantles unnecessary hierarchical structures and promotes a flat platform where interaction, innovation, and growth are possible for everyone involved. This form of interaction creates a space that nourishes the collective intellect, inspiring creativity and catalyzing a synergy that sees the team move as a single, cohesive, and incredibly potent unit.

6.6. The Odyssean Journey: Navigating towards the Horizon of Ego-less Leadership

Adopting the model of ego-less leadership is not a one-time event but an odyssean journey requiring consistent commitment, courage, and compassion. Courage to relinquish personal ego, commitment to remain mindful, and compassion to foster a deep-seated connection with your colleagues – these are the three pillars supporting your journey toward a new horizon of leadership.

En route, reassess your leadership strategies, realign your approaches with the values of fearless leadership, and rejuvenate your teams by inspiring them to embrace a work-life grounded in humility, authenticity, and empathy.

Unburdened by ego, a new breed of fearless, ego-less leaders is emerging, ready to propel their organizations into uncharted territories of sustainable success and growth. The transformation starts with you, from within you. Unleash the power of Fearless Leadership, dare to be the change that your organization needs. To a reimagined, transformed, and fearlessly successful you!

Chapter 7. Solutions in Harmony: Co-Creation and Client-Centered Strategies

The fulcrum of any sustainable and effective business strategy hinges on the principles of co-creation and client-centricity. By forging a collaborative environment where problem-solving and creativity thrive, solutions that reflect the needs and expectations of the client can be crafted seamlessly. Imbibing the spirit of harmony and coalescence, this chapter delves into embodying these principles within your own strategic framework, thus fostering an ecosystem of shared responsibility and innovation.

7.1. Discovering Co-Creation: The Power of Collective Wisdom

Co-creation does not merely refer to a collaborative endeavor between two parties but is an exploration of collective power, mutual respect, and shared goals. It emphasizes the inclusive process of business solution formation, from preliminary conception to execution and evaluation.

The co-creation process involves gathering various stakeholders - your team, your clients, and your strategic partners. Together, each participant contributes their valuable insights and perspectives, creating a fertile ground for innovative thinking and problem resolution. This inclusive approach ensures that every participant feels heard and validated, encouraging the growth of trust, commitment, and a strong network.

7.2. Fabric of Co-Creation: Inclusion, Transparency, and Shared Responsibility

Inclusion implies the active participation of all stakeholders, ensuring diverse perspectives. Transparency calls for open communication channels and mutual understanding. While shared responsibility encourages ownership and engagement. These are the key pillars that uphold the fabric of co-creation.

The inclusivity ensures that each participant's unique insight is integrated into solution crafting. Hence, diversity in the co-creation process stimulates innovation. Transparency, on the other hand, fortifies the trust and resilience of the co-creative team, allowing these synergic relationships to thrive even in challenging times. Lastly, shared responsibility paves the way for higher levels of commitment and engagement.

7.3. Client-Centricity: Meeting the Ambitions of Today and Tomorrow

Client-centricity is a paradigm wherein your clients' needs and aspirations are placed at the core of your business strategy. Amidst a rapidly evolving business climate, understanding these shifting needs becomes pivotal for delivering optimal client satisfaction.

When co-creation marries client-centricity, a unique intersection is found where the clients become active contributors in the solution-crafting journey, thus ensuring personalized path in the best interest of the client. The result is a tailored solution that is in-tune with evolving client expectations and market trends.

7.4. Co-Creation and Client-Centricity: Bridging the Gap

The potent combination of co-creation and client-centricity turns conventional consulting models on their heads. While traditional models may view the consultancy and clients as separate entities, this approach emphasizes a symbiotic relationship. Bridging this gap leads to a market-responsive consulting model that out-performs traditional methods.

7.5. The Co-Creation Cycle

1. Ideation Phase: Begin with brainstorming sessions that encourage all participants to share their thoughts and ideas. This creates a melting pot of creative solutions.

ii. Design Phase: By using client input, design proposals for problem resolution that are customized to client needs and expectations.

iii. Evaluation Phase: Gather collective input to analyze the effectiveness of the design. Feedback is key as it allows for adjustments and improvements specific to each situation.

iv. Execution Phase: With a designed solution in hand, it is implemented while maintaining open communication channels and incorporating any necessary changes.

1. Follow-up Phase: Regular follow-ups to ensure the solution continues to provide value to the client.

7.6. Embracing Disruptive Innovation

The merger of co-creation and client-centricity is changing the future face of consulting. By acknowledging each stakeholder's value and eradicating barriers that hinder communication and mutual respect, this strategy encourages disruptive innovation. Embracing such a fearless approach will ensure a thriving, sustainable, and successful future.

Keep in mind, disruption is no enemy. It is merely a pathway towards new solutions, increased efficiency, and better ways of servicing your clients.

7.7. Navigating the Challenges

There are inherent challenges in implementing this approach. The fear of change, overcoming ego, dispelling hierarchy, and fostering an environment of utter transparency can be daunting. However, mindfulness and relentless commitment will ensure successful navigation of these rough seas.

This journey is not linear. It involves constant learning and growth, and an unwavering dedication to placing your clients' needs at the heart of your services and solutions. Embrace these challenges as stepping stones towards your own fearless future. As in the course of evolution, it is the fittest who survive.

As we march forward into this new era of consulting services, grasping the power of co-creation and client-centric solutions is key to unlocking unprecedented potential and an exciting frontier of sustainable success.

Chapter 8. The Resilience Recipe: Building a Pandemic-Proof Business

The entire planet has been shaken by the unprecedented impact of the COVID-19 pandemic. It has wreaked havoc on the standard business model, leaving ashes of shattered plans and disrupted schedules in its wake. However, amidst the chaos, we are also learning valuable lessons. One of them is the importance of building a resilient business: one that is strong enough to withstand the hottest fires of global crisis and emerge steel-like — stronger, more robust, and unyieldingly reliable.

8.1. Resilience: The Ultimate Business Buzzword

Resilience, more than ever before, has earned its place in the entrepreneurial dictionary. With its metaphorical prowess, resilience forms the bedrock of enterprises capable of surviving tumultuous circumstances. It's the ultimate indicator of adaptability, signifying an organization's capacity to absorb shocks, confront challenges head-on, and continually evolve.

The importance of resilience is not forgotten during periods of calm either. During "peacetime," businesses that prioritize resilience strengthen their core operations and readiness, ensuring that when storms roll in, the ground beneath their feet stands unswayed.

8.2. The Fundamental Elements of a Resilient Business

As consultants, when we step into an organization, we assess several key factors that contribute to resilience. These include the business's structure, culture, adaptability to change, robustness in risk management, and, at a deeper level, the level of mindfulness nurtured in its ecosystem.

8.2.1. Structural Resilience

Structural resilience refers to the robustness of a company's architecture — its work processes, systems, principles, and policies. It demands efficient contingency planning, functional redundancy, and a level of decentralization that allows local units to operate even if the central system encounters challenges.

8.2.2. Cultural Resilience

A resilient culture is one that encourages open communication, values trust and cooperation, fosters learning and development, appreciates diverse perspectives, and maintains a committed workforce. It allows for a supportive, trust-based environment that not only helps in building strong teams, but that also reacts positively to crisis situations.

8.2.3. Adaptive Resilience

The ability to adapt to changing circumstances is a key predictor of an organization's resilience. This recognizes the importance of agility and flexibility in modifying operational strategies based on emerging developments, providing a competitive advantage in the ever-changing business environment.

8.2.4. Risk Management

Robust risk management underpins resilience. This begins with understanding the business landscape, identifying potential threats, evaluating their impact, and creating mitigation strategies.

8.2.5. Mindfulness

The role of mindfulness in cultivating resilience often goes unacknowledged. It enables us to maintain a sense of balance, awareness, and concentration amidst adversity, reducing reactivity and enhancing thoughtful and measured responses.

8.3. Building a Pandemic-Proof, Resilient Business

A resilient business does more than just survive during times of crisis—it evolves and even thrives. The following steps based on the key elements outlined earlier can guide organizations to become pandemic-proof.

8.3.1. Create Robust Structural Systems

In this era of uncertainty, businesses need systems that can absorb shocks. Invest in cloud-based technology, VPNs for secure remote access, and project management tools to keep teams connected and organized. Create emergency response plans tailored to potential crisis scenarios, ensuring business continuity during disruptions.

8.3.2. Nurture a Resilient Culture

Businesses should foster a culture of resilience by prioritizing well-being, mental health, and maintaining open lines of communication. Leaders who display a growth mindset and encourage constructive feedback foster a culture of continuous learning and adaptability.

8.3.3. Enhance Adaptability

Ensure your business is adaptable, ready to pivot at any point. This includes embracing digital transformations, adopting remote work models, and speeding up decision-making processes. Building a culture of innovation encourages experimentation and helps businesses stay ahead of the curve.

8.3.4. Prioritize Comprehensive Risk Management

Identify potential threats and determine their impact on your business. Develop comprehensive risk mitigation strategies that consider every facet of the organization. This not only includes the financial aspect, but also the impact on employees, stakeholders, and the supply chain.

8.3.5. Cultivate Mindfulness in the Organization

Promoting mindfulness at every level of an organization helps to enhance emotional intelligence and improve decision-making abilities. It fosters a deep sense of empathy and connection with the team, which can be especially helpful during times of crisis.

8.4. Recalibrating for a Post-Pandemic Landscape

The pandemic has changed the way businesses operate. Measures taken for survival during these challenging times may morph into permanent strategies. Work-from-home routines might become ubiquitous. Digital transformations could be more widely accepted, creating new norms in every organizational sphere.

Building a resilient business is a continuous journey. It starts with the recognition of crisis, then the response, recovery, and finally resilience. By adapting to the emerging pandemic-driven realities, organizations can set a course for sustainable growth in the post-pandemic future. They can become veritable pillars of resilience, illuminating the way amidst the storm for other enterprises to follow.

The goal of achieving resilience for a pandemic-proof business is the ability to weather the storms of today, but it can also serve as a catalyst for flourishing in the calm periods of tomorrow. The journey is not about reaching a destination where everything is unchangeable; instead, it's about continuously improving and evolving, meeting challenges with creativity, innovation, and adaptability, and paving the way for a sustainable, successful future.

Chapter 9. Innovation for Sustainability: Navigating through Change

It has been evident for years that transformations in business practices are not just crucial to maximise profits but also to explore the latest concepts in sustainability and responsible growth. In this context, understanding, accepting, and implementing the term "Innovation for Sustainability" has never been as essential as it is today.

9.1. The Age of Sustainability: Understanding the Connection

Sustainability is not just a buzzword or a trend; it is a necessity and a commitment towards our planet. In the business world, sustainability means adopting business strategies and activities that meet the needs of the enterprise and its stakeholders while protecting and enhancing the human and natural resources that will be needed in the future.

Innovation, on the other hand, is a productive process involving the practical implementation of an idea that ultimately improves upon or makes a significant contribution to existing products, processes, or services. It becomes a symbiotic half of our overarching term when seen in combination with sustainability.

Companies that innovate for sustainability view the constraints posed by environmental and social issues not as hindrances but as opportunities to create new markets, reduce costs, and enhance reputation and brand equity.

9.2. Designing a Sustainable Business Model: Steps Towards Innovation

Creating a sustainable business model requires an understanding of the different elements that play a role and how they are interconnected. Here, we explore the four main steps involved in designing a business model focused on sustainability:

1. Understand the Landscape: Awareness and understanding of industry norms, emerging trends, and stakeholder expectations allow a business to identify opportunities and threats within its environment.

2. Define the Value Proposition: This entails deciding on your business's purpose or 'reason for being'. Uncovering the unique product or service offerings that are geared towards sustainability is critical at this stage.

3. Design the Value Architecture: This step involves structuring the business's activities that deliver on the value proposition, as well as managing the key partnerships needed to execute the value proposition.

4. Build Profit Formula: The financial aspect of the business model that calculates the margin, resource velocity, and scale needed to generate a profit sustainable in the long term.

9.3. The Role of Mindfulness in Sustainability-Driven Innovation

The role of mindfulness in promoting sustainability-driven innovation is founded on the concept that aligning one's attention and awareness to the present moment fosters a deeper understanding of the interconnectedness of all things, an ethical concern for other people, and the future of our planet.

Mindfulness supports sustainability in three essential ways:

1. Enhancing Focus on Long-Term Outcomes: Mindfulness nurtures a long-term perspective and helps us to avoid being steered by short-term gains.

2. Cultivating Ethical Decision-Making: Mindful people display a heightened sense of responsibility, essential for making decisions that uphold sustainability and create a positive societal impact.

3. Boosting Creativity: Mindfulness trains the brain to become more flexible, which is necessary to leave comfort zones, imagine new possibilities, and drive Innovation for Sustainability.

9.4. Nudging Businesses toward Sustainable Innovation

One means to spur companies into action is by 'nudging' – subtly encouraging or persuading individuals or organizations to make specific choices or behave in particular ways. Several strategies can be employed:

1. Making Sustainability the Default: The human brain prefers to accept the default option. Creating default choices that favor sustainability encourages businesses to do what's right without imposing regulations or restrictions.

2. Framing Sustainability Positively: Emphasizing the benefits of sustainability, such as reduced operating costs, improved reputation, and customer loyalty, can effectively motivate organizations.

3. Using Social Norms: People are innately influenced by what others do. Displaying evidence of other organizations embracing sustainability can prompt similar behavior in others.

In the era of global challenges, each business has the power to make a difference. Innovation for Sustainability requires a shift in perspective, a deep understanding, and strategic implementation of sustainable practices, and the courage to break away from the status quo. Adopting these features will not only lead to a more prosperous future but a healthier and happier Earth for generations to come. As we look forward towards uncharted territories, remember: the only constant is change. So let's navigate through it mindfully, innovatively, and sustainably.

Chapter 10. The Sound of Silence: The Importance of Reflective Listening in Consulting

In the tumultuous world of consulting, filled with fact-filled presentations, pitches aimed at convincing powerful decision-makers, and non-stop, high-pressure engagements, taking time to listen - truly and deeply - can be a lost skill. Given the pace and urgency of consulting assignments, how can we pause long enough to listen? Why is it important? When we typically think of 'silence,' we may associate it with nothingness, emptiness, or inactivity. But what if 'silence' could be viewed as a space filled with untapped insights, reflective understanding, and perceptive mindfulness?

10.1. The Art & Science of Listening

To understand reflective listening, we must first learn to appreciate the importance of 'listening' itself. The renowned scholar Carl Rogers once said, "When someone really hears you without passing judgment on you, without trying to take responsibility for you, without trying to mold you, it feels damn good!" Isn't it amazing how such a seemingly straightforward act can arouse profound feelings of appreciation and validation?

Most of us believe we are inherently good listeners. But the truth is, proper listening requires effort and practice. It goes beyond hearing the spoken words. It involves perceiving the underlying emotions, understanding the implicit ideas, and developing a sense of the speaker's personal context.

In consulting, listening helps us understand our clients' real needs. It aids in developing customized strategies that address unique challenges. It constructs a foundation of goodwill and trust, vital elements for any successful consultation process.

10.2. Taking Listening to a Reflective Level

Moving from simple listening to reflective listening entails an enhanced level of engagement. Reflective listening involves introspection and feedback. It requires the listener not only to understand the speaker's message but also to mirror or echo it back to them. This type of listening fosters the speaker's sense of being understood, a factor that can greatly bolster the consulting relationship.

Reflective listening is the crux of empathic understanding and is significant to the consulting sphere for several compelling reasons. By practicing reflective listening, consultants can forge a deeper connection with clients, fostering a psychologically safe environment wherein clients feel comfortable expressing their thoughts, ideas, fears, and ambitions.

10.3. Using Silence as a Tool

Just as music is made not only of notes but also of the silence between them, reflective listening is as much about the moments of quiet introspection as it is about echoing the speaker's sentiments. Silence and listening go hand in hand. Silence gives us time to filter, comprehend, and resonate with the speaker's thoughts. This is the period when we make sense of what we hear - a critical stage for a consultant aiming to provide a reasoned, value-creating response.

While silence creates a canvas for reflective listening, it also accomplishes other essential tasks. Significant among these are:

1. Providing time to think: Both for the listener, who digests the information, and the speaker, who can collect thoughts and articulate more clearly.

2. Revealing the unsaid: Silence can indicate disagreement, discomfort or a gap in understanding. As a consultant, observing these silent moments helps draw attention to potential issues and work on them proactively.

3. Facilitating reflection: Encouraging the speaker to delve deeper into their thoughts and solidifying their perspectives and ideas.

10.4. Pacing to the Rhythm of Dialogue

Consultants must adapt to the conversational rhythm where reflective listening can effectively thrive. The "Rhythm of Dialogue" is a technique wherein consultants alternate between periods of listening, reflecting, and speaking, promoting a balanced conversation that benefits everyone involved.

This rhythm fuels better decision-making. It encourages leaders to consider multiple perspectives and suggestions, leading to well-rounded, insightful decisions. This inclusive, collaborative model cultivates a culture of shared responsibility and collective success.

10.5. Anchoring Reflective Listening into Consulting Practices

To anchor reflective listening into consulting practices, remember these key aspects:

1. Train yourself to listen: As with any new habit formation, beginning can be the most challenging part. Practice genuinely listening to colleagues, friends, or family. Gradually, it will

become second nature.

2. Be patient: Reflective listening requires patience. It's about the quality of understanding, not the speed of conversation.

3. Encourage open dialogues: Construct meetings and discussions that make room for reflective listening. Allow silences. Promote thought and idea exchanges instead of mere information delivery.

4. Incorporate feedback loop: Include a feedback stage in your conversation for verification and clarification, ensuring everyone is on the same page.

In conclusion, reflective listening, bolstered by mindful silences and understanding, can become an invaluable tool in a consultant's toolkit. By incorporating this practice, consultants can foster stronger relationships, develop more tailored solutions, and ultimately, drive greater client satisfaction and success. And all this starts with the power of silence - a skill as vital as it is overlooked. May this realization guide us to a future where we not only speak but listen to create value, drive change, and shape better businesses and communities.

Chapter 11. Mapping the Journey Ahead: Your Toolkit for a Fearless Future

Small yet definitive steps, when consistently taken, can lead to massive changes. In our quest for a fearless future and transformative growth, we must equip ourselves with the right tools to navigate uncharted territories with confidence. The following toolkit offers strategies and methodologies to achieve just that.

11.1. Building your Navigator's Compass

Navigating your journey into a fearless future begins by building a Navigator's Compass. This is a unique blend of strategic tools and mindful practices, which are designed to guide you steadily through corporate transformations.

11.1.1. Strategic Tools

Strategic tools refer to analytical models and consulting frameworks that will help explore various business dimensions. SWOT analysis, McKinsey's 7S Framework, and Porter's Five Forces, among others, provide a 360-degree view of current potentials and challenges. Use these methodologies to understand your organization's current standing, its economic environment, market competition, internal strengths and weaknesses, and anticipated threats and opportunities.

11.1.2. Mindful Practices

Mindful practices, on the other hand, offer resilience against the stress of change. Techniques such as mindful listening, meditation, and presence practices bring about calm, focus, and clarity, enabling more apt decision-making. These practices contribute to creating an environment of trust, empathy, and openness. Weaving mindfulness into your strategic processes promotes an ego-less leadership style that is both inclusive and transformational.

11.2. Crafting your Change Map

Our next instrument is envisaging a Change Map. It offers the roadmap to your desired future. It keeps you on track, showing milestones and checkpoints along your journey to keep a tab on progress.

11.2.1. Visioning

Start with creating a Vision Statement. It should be aspirational yet attainable. It should articulate your organization's goal for the future, igniting the passion and motivation of everyone involved. Work on defining your organizational purpose, the 'why' behind your operations.

11.2.2. Missioning

Next, define the mission. It should describe what you will be doing to bring your vision into reality. Break down the vision into tangible actions. By making your aspirations actionable, you transform your organizational desires into specific initiatives.

11.2.3. Goal-setting

Lastly, set measurable goals. These should be realistic, quantifiable objectives that your team is striving to achieve. Ensure there are Key Performance Indicators (KPIs) tied to the goals, as this helps track progress and maintains focus on the desired outcomes.

11.3. Cultivating your Cultural Ecosystem

The third tool in our kit is Cultivating your Cultural Ecosystem. It focuses on creating an organizational culture that thrives on co-creation, collaboration, and a client-centred approach.

11.3.1. Core values

Define your core values as they set the tone for how your organization will function and interact both internally and externally. Whether those are transparency, integrity, or inclusivity, these values form the backbone of your cultural ecosystem.

11.3.2. Emotional Intelligence

Foster Emotional Intelligence (EQ) within teams as EQ enhances interpersonal relationships and boosts mental resilience. This facilitates better teamwork and boosts productivity.

11.3.3. Agile Mindset

Instill an Agile Mindset. As the pace of change accelerates, Agile provides an advanced framework for dealing with uncertainty and ambiguity while maintaining a customer-centric approach.

11.4. Nurturing Continuous Learning

The final tool emphasizes the importance of Nurturing Continuous Learning. To stay relevant in this dynamic world, continuous learning and adaptation are crucial.

11.4.1. Personal Development Plans

Individuals must have Personal Development Plans (PDPs) that align with the vision of the organization. These plans help in identifying areas each team member needs to develop further in, thus enhancing overall competence.

11.4.2. Training programs

Implement ongoing training and development programs to keep your team adaptable and innovative. Include both hard and soft skills, catering to the all-round development of the personnel.

11.4.3. Knowledge Sharing

Promote knowledge sharing. Encourage employees to share their experiential learning and insights, sparking conversations that can lead to new ideas and fresh perspectives.

11.4.4. Feedback Cultivation

Instigate a culture of continuous feedback. Constructive feedback contributes to learning and growth, fostering a culture of continuous improvement and mutual respect.

Equip yourself with this toolkit and set sail on an exciting journey towards a fearless future. It's a comprehensive guide to navigating the changing tides of the business landscape. While tools can help us prepare, there is no substitute for the commitment, dedication, and passion required to achieve true transformation and sustainable success. Invest in this powerful transformation tool, and embrace the consulting norms of tomorrow, today. Your fearless future awaits!